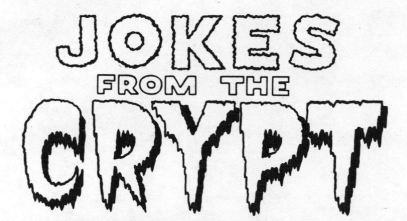

JOKES FROM THE CRYPT

Told by the Vault-Keeper, the Old Witch, and the Crypt-Keeper

with the assistance of
ELEANOR FREMONT

text illustrations by
ARISTIDES RUIZ

A TALES FROM THE CRYPT BOOK

Bullseye Books™
Random House 🏠 New York

A BULLSEYE BOOK PUBLISHED BY RANDOM HOUSE, INC.

Library of Congress Cataloging-in-Publication Data
Fremont, Eleanor. Jokes from the crypt / told by the Crypt-Keeper, the
Vault-Keeper, and the Old Witch, with the assistance of Eleanor Fremont ;
text illustrations by Aristides Ruiz.
     p. cm. "A Tales from the crypt book."
SUMMARY: A collection of jokes featuring vampires, werewolves, and other
grisly characters.
ISBN 0-679-83168-1 (pbk.)
1. Wit and humor, Juvenile. [1. Monsters—Wit and humor. 2. Jokes.]
I. Ruiz, Aristides, ill. II. Fremont, Eleanor. Tales from the crypt.
III. Title. PN6163.F74 1992 818'.5402—dc20 92-4056

First Bullseye Books edition: 1993

Manufactured in the United States of America

10 9 8 7 6 5 4 3 2

CONTENTS

This book is dedicated to

WILLIAM M. GAINES

1922–1992

INTRODUCTION

*Greetings and salivations, boils and drools!
It's nice to have you in our clutches again.
Because we have something to tell you.
Something very important.*

*It has recently come to our attention that
you consider us creepy. That you think the
three of us are a moldy old bunch of perverts
who sit around all day, putrefying and
growing fungus and being boring.*

*Well, we are here to tell you that you are
wrong. In fact, you have made a grave error.
Perhaps there is a fungus among us. Maybe
there is a little mold in our fold. And perhaps*

we _are_ odoriferous and ugly. But boring—
never!

We are, in fact, a funny, funny trio—
regular party animals. And to prove to you
how very funny we can be, we have dredged
up a select group of our favorite chokes—er,
jokes—for you. More than a _gross_ of them.
There are jokes to match any mood you're in,
whether it be rancid, foul, or just plain
unpleasant.

Like werewolves? We have werewolf jokes
that are an absolute howl. Into murder? We
have murderer jokes that'll slay you. Think
Dracula's dreamy? We have vampire jokes
that—well, we'll stick our necks out and say
that these are jokes in a very, very humorous
vein.

And that's not all. Here are jokes with
which you can torture your teacher, browbeat
your brother, and make your friends afraid.

So next time you're tempted to think of us
as just a bunch of festering old fuddy-

duddies, *think again. We're an absolute* scream.

As you read this book, you'll notice that each one of us is hosting a special section for you. That way, you can judge for yourself which of us has the most sparkling wit.

Well, good-bye for now. It's time for our favorite TV rerun: I Dismember Mama.

> *Your faithful fiends,*
> *The Vault-Keeper ("Vaulty")*
> *The Old Witch ("Fran")*
> *The Crypt-Keeper ("Crypty")*

WICKED WITTICISMS OF THE MISUNDERSTOOD BUT OH-SO DEBONAIR VAULT-KEEPER

 *Greetings, kiddies. Why, look how big you are. I do believe you gruesome since I saw you last. I'm sure that means you're old enough to enjoy the very sophisticated jokes I've chosen for your enjoyment. You see, unlike those cackling, cadaverous clowns the Crypt-Keeper and the Old Witch, who'll do anything for a laugh, I have an <u>appreciation</u> of fine culture—of the <u>art</u> of comedy. I suppose it's only natural. I'm the oldest, after all. I have at least two centuries on both of them. And so, with my great powers of discrimination, I've chosen jokes that even a cannibal would find . . . tasteful. Chow!*

*Refinedly yours,
The Vault-Keeper*

Old Witch: "I just had a wart removed
          from my nose."

Vault-Keeper: "Have a scar?"

Old Witch: "No, thank you. I don't
          smoke."

What do you call a person who eats only
human flesh?

        A humanitarian.

THAT WAS A MOLDY OLDIE!

KINDLY BUTT OUT OF MY SECTION!

Why did the Cyclops give up teaching?

> Because he only had one pupil.

What do you call a mortician's place of business?

> A box office.

Ghoul child: "Daddy, is it OK to eat chicken legs with my fingers?"

Ghoul father: "No, it is not! Fingers should *always* be eaten separately!"

What happens to authors when they die?

They become ghost writers.

What did the mortician sing after a particularly nice funeral?

> "Oh, What a Beautiful
> Mourning!"

Teacher: "Tell me all you know about the
        Dead Sea."
Student: "I don't know anything! I didn't
        even know it was sick!"

What happened to the girl who swallowed a spoon?

> She didn't stir.

What did the missionaries give the cannibals?

> Their first taste of Christianity.

What is the most difficult part of mortuary school?

The stiff exams.

What do you call a graverobber who works shipwrecks?

A sea ghoul.

Did you hear about the laborer who worked with hundreds of people under him?

He mowed the lawn in a cemetery.

Why did the evil chicken cross the road?

> For a fowl reason.

What is the difference between a vampire with a fang ache and a thunderstorm?

> One roars with pain and the other pours with rain.

Why did the boy take an aspirin after hearing a werewolf howl?

> Because it gave him an eerie ache.

What do you get when a vampire bites a rat?

> A neighborhood without cats.

Passenger: "This ship is sinking!"

Captain: "That's correct, madam. But you
needn't worry. We're only a
mile from land."

Passenger: "A mile! In what direction!"

Captain: "Down."

What kind of typewriter do vampires like best?

One that types blood.

Why are there fences around graveyards?

Because so many people are dying to get in.

Why are executioners so unpopular?

> Because they're always hanging around.

What happens when you fail to pay an exorcist?

> You get repossessed.

Why did the vampire win an art scholarship?

> Because of the way he drew blood.

What did one casket say to the other?

> "Is that you coffin?"

Where do hangmen look for jobs?

> In the noosepaper.

Old Witch: "You must come over and see my new dog!"

Vault-Keeper: "Does he bite?"

Old Witch: "That's what I'd like to find out."

Sign above doorway in funeral parlor:

Coroner's assistant: "Can I bring a guest to watch your next autopsy?"

Coroner: "Of course! The morgue the merrier!"

How did the werewolf feel after eating the goose?

> Down in the mouth.

Where do you find vampire snails?

> On the ends of vampire's fingers.

Crypt-Keeper: "I hear zombies avoid cemeteries."

Vault-Keeper: "Yes, they wouldn't be caught dead there."

What do liars do when they die?

They lie still.

What do you call someone who thinks he's a big black bird?

A raven maniac.

Sign outside funeral parlor:

TRY OUR LAY AWAY PLAN

Vault-Keeper: "My ex-wife was a medium."

Crypt-Keeper: "Really? Mine was a small."

Sign outside a crematorium:

URN MORE—PAY LESS!

Who digs graves during a gravedigger strike?

A skeleton crew.

What did one Egyptian mummy say to the other?

"I can't recall your name, but your fez is familiar."

Crypt-Keeper: "Have you ever seen the Catskill Mountains?"

Vault-Keeper: "No. But I've seen them kill birds and mice."

Vault-Keeper: "My father can imitate a sparrow."

Crypt-Keeper: "Really? How does he do that?"

Vault-Keeper: "He pulls a worm out of the ground with his teeth and eats it."

Old Witch: "Morgues are *so* unpopular!"

Vault-Keeper: "Yes, they leave most people cold."

How did the gravedigger get his job?

He fell into it.

What do ghouls learn to write in school?

Death sentences.

Crypt-Keeper: "My father died from
              drinking furniture polish."

Vault-Keeper: "Yes, but what a fine finish
              he had!"

Ghost #1: "What is the hardest thing
           about learning to skydive?"

Ghost #2: "The ground."

How did the undertaker carry his lunch to the park?

In a picnic casket.

"Doctor, I think I'm turning into a werewolf!"

"Sit!"

What did the man on death row want for dessert at his last meal?

A Life Saver.

Undertaker: "I'm afraid I buried your father in the wrong plot."

Bereaved: "That was a grave mistake."

Why did the boy bury his bowling
trophy?

Because he wanted it engraved.

"Help! I've swallowed a bone!"

"Are you choking?"

"No, I'm serious!"

Where do you take an Egyptian mummy
with a bad back?

      To a Cairo-practor.

What happens when you swallow a lazy
Susan?

      Your stomach turns.

Old Witch: "All my life I've had men falling at my feet."

Vault-Keeper: "Yes—podiatrists."

"Excuse me, Captain, but do these planes crash very often?"

"No. As a rule, they only crash once."

"Doctor, Doctor! I've swallowed a clock!"

"There's no need to get
alarmed."

What do you call a dead parrot?

    A polygon.

What goes in pink and comes out blue?

    A body in a freezer.

What do you do with a dead cow?

    Cream-ate it.

What do you get if you cross the Loch
Ness Monster with a great white shark?

    Loch Jaws.

What do an electric chair and a period
have in common?

    They both end a sentence.

What do you call a shaggy dead sporting dog?

A croaker spaniel.

What did Tutankhamen call his parents?
Mummy and Deady.

Vaulty: "Speaking of Tut, did you know I
can trace my ancestry back to
royalty?"

Crypty: "Who, King Kong?"

Vault-Keeper: "What has four legs and
one arm?"

Crypt-Keeper: "A pit bull?"

Jonah: "Daddy, I'm seasick."

Father: "But we're home, son. Not at sea."

Jonah: "I know. But everything I see
makes me sick."

What kind of car does a vampire drive?

A bloodmobile.

"Splendid stuffed tiger you have there, old boy."

"So kind of you to notice. Uncle Reggie bagged it on expedition in India."

"Whatever is it stuffed with?"

"Uncle Reggie."

THE I-CAN-SAY-ANYTHING-BECAUSE-I'M-BEAUTIFUL-AND-ALLURING REPARTEE OF THE OLD WITCH

Welcome to <u>my</u> section, you juicy little morsels. It's time you let a real woman tell you some jokes. You know, the feminine touch is very important in humor—for instance, in jokes about <u>men</u>. I love a good joke about a man, don't you? Of course, a lot of the ones I've included here are very personal, because they're about vampires, werewolves, and ghouls I have known. In fact, some of them have been—how shall I say it?—<u>very close friends</u> of mine. (In four hundred years, you have time to rack up quite a lot of relationships.) And speaking of relationships, it's time for me to get ready for my big date. I

hate to boast, but it won't take much for me to wrap Big Foot around my little finger. A sip of my vintage frog chardonnay, a taste of my succulent newt-eye stew . . . and a few really good Neanderthal jokes should do it. Or my name isn't—

> *"Fran"*
> *The Old*
> *Witch*

What do you call a corpse that's been buried a long time?

Pete.

Vaulty: "Did you hear about the waiter at the asylum?"

Crypty: "Yeah, he served soup to nuts."

How does an ax murderer count the time before Christmas?

In chopping days.

Graverobber #1: "That's a great jacket you're wearing."

Graverobber #2: "Thanks. It's just a little something I dug up."

What always follows a werewolf?

Its tail.

Which side of a werewolf has the most fur?

The outside.

Why did the murderer chop up his victims?

So they could rest in pieces.

What have you got when a zombie presses your doorbell?

A dead ringer.

Why do vampires make cheap dinner
dates?

> Because they eat necks to
> nothing.

Why did the witch use radioactive cold cream at night?

So she could wake up with a glowing complexion.

What kind of a necklace does a strangler give his girlfriend?

A choker.

How do you keep a werewolf from charging?

Cut up its credit cards.

Why do fortune-tellers love their work?

Because they have a ball.

"Mommy! Mommy! What's a werewolf?"

"Shut up and comb your face."

What do mummies do on vacation?

They unwind.

Why did the girl lock her father in a freezer?

Because she wanted an ice pop.

Why are demons so popular with ghouls?

> Because demons are a ghoul's
> best friend.

Crypt-Keeper: "Fran, how did you lose
your first husband?"

Old Witch: "Illness."

Crypt-Keeper: "What kind of illness?"

Old Witch: "I got sick of him!"

Why do spiders spin webs?

> Because they can't crochet.

Why did the man bury his wife up to her
waist?

> Because she said she felt
> half-dead.

What do you call a row of zombies?

A deadline.

Why did the werewolf laugh after chewing a bone?

It was a funny bone.

What did the vampire say after he bit his victim's neck?

"It's been nice gnawing you."

What do vampires like best about country life?

The rednecks.

What position did the graverobber play
on the hockey team?

Ghoulie.

What did the Headless Horseman say
when given a comb as a gift?

"I will never part with this."

Teacher: "Jane, what would Abe Lincoln be doing if he were alive today?"

Jane: "Scratching at the lid of his coffin!"

Vault-Keeper: "Your cough sounds much better today."

Old Witch: "Thanks. I was up all night practicing."

Why don't skeletons play music in church?

They have no organs.

Crypt-Keeper: "What do you do when a woman rolls her eyes at you?"

Vault-Keeper: "A gentleman picks them up and rolls them back."

What do you call a skeleton who plays in the snow without any clothes on?

A numb skull.

What do you get when you cross a ghost with a cow?

Vanishing cream.

What does a dead rooster crow in the morning?

Cock-a-doodle-*boo!*

Why did the ghoul call the funeral parlor?

>To see if they deliver.

Why didn't the skeleton go to the prom?

>Because he had no body to go with.

Why did the werewolf go to the orthodontist?

> To improve his bite.

Old Witch: "Since appearing on stage with my magic act, I've received several intriguing offers."

Vault-Keeper: "From plastic surgeons?"

What is a vampire's favorite fruit?

A nectarine.

Why won't vampires drink chicken blood?

Because it's fowl-tasting.

What is a vampire's favorite animal?

    The giraffe.

What happened to the cannibal after he
ate the comedian?

    He felt funny.

What is the leading cause of death among vampires?

Tooth decay.

What happened after the werewolf swallowed the clock?

He got ticks.

What do you get when you put a live rabbit into a toaster oven?

A hot cross bunny.

What did the cannibal podiatrist eat for breakfast?

Corn flakes.

"Mommy, Mommy! Am I really a vampire?"

    "Shut up and drink your soup before it clots!"

Why did the rooster cross the road during rush hour?

    To show the chicken he had guts.

Warning printed on witch broomstick:

DON'T FLY OFF THE
HANDLE!

Why did the witches unionize?

Because they wanted sweeping
reforms.

Crypt-Keeper: "I saw a man-eating shark in the water."

Vault-Keeper: "That's nothing! I saw a man eating pie in the cafeteria."

Old Witch: "Have you heard about the sword swallower who went on a diet?"

Crypt-Keeper: "No."

Old Witch: "He was on pins and needles for five weeks."

What did one vampire say to the other?

"Let's step out for a bite!"

Who do ghouls like to play with?

Any body they can dig up.

Cowboy: "What a great new branding
        iron this is!"

Cow: "Yes. I'm very impressed!"

"I'm bored, Ma."

"Well, go outside and play with Grandpa."

"Awww...I dug *him* up yesterday!"

Why did the farmer scream?

        Someone stepped on his corn.

Old Witch: "I had to have my dog put to
        sleep yesterday."

Vault-Keeper: "Was he mad?"

Old Witch: "He wasn't pleased!"

How can you tell a hamster from a bowl of linguine?

> The hamster won't slip off your fork.

How do you keep a corpse from smelling?

> Cut off its nose.

Why didn't the werewolf jump through the screen door?

He didn't want to strain himself.

What note do you hear when a coal mine collapses?

A flat miner.

Why did the woman shoot her husband with a bow and arrow?

So she wouldn't wake the children.

What do you call a vampire who works 24 hours a day?

An all-day sucker.

What do you get if you cross poison ivy with a black cat?

A rash of bad luck.

How did the man feel when he was
suddenly hit by lightning?

Shocked.

COSMIC CACKLE FROM THE RICH AND FAMOUS BUT STILL DEEPLY SPIRITUAL AND POLITICALLY CORRECT CRYPT-KEEPER

Hi there, groovy dudes. What's happening? I'll bet you've been just <u>dying</u> to get to my section. You know that a cool guy like me is going to have the coolest jokes. Hey, just because I live in a crypt doesn't mean I'm out of it. I'm in touch! I'm hip! Because, dig it, I'm a lot younger than those other two—I'm only three hundred and twenty-eight. Like, I can <u>relate</u>. I don't have a bunch of moldy old jokes, I have a bunch of moldy <u>new</u> jokes.

So let's get down and go with the flow. Are these jokes going to flip you out? Of corpse!

Rest in peace, man,
The Crypt-Keeper

What do vampires learn in math class?

Blood counts.

What do you call a demonically possessed motorbike?

A vicious cycle.

What's the difference between Bruce Springsteen and a corpse?

> One composes and the other decomposes.

Ghoul #1: "I hate the teacher."

Ghoul #2: "I don't like her either. Maybe ketchup would help?"

Vault-Keeper: "How can you tell if someone has a glass eye?"

Crypt-Keeper: "It usually comes out in conversation."

Witch: "Give me my hand back!"

Crypty: "Aww, I thought you wanted to be my ghoulfriend."

When should you suspect a chicken of being demonically possessed?

When it uses fowl language.

How do you disguise a mummy?

With masking tape.

How do you make a werewolf stew?

Keep him waiting for two
hours.

Why do people hate getting bitten by
vampires?

Because it's a drain in the neck.

"Daddy! Daddy! When can we buy a garbage can?"

"Shut up and keep eating!"

What do you call a person who sticks his right hand into a great white shark's mouth?

Lefty.

Vaulty: "What do you call a person who listens to Crypty's jokes?"

Witch: "Sleepy."

Vaulty: "Or maybe Grumpy?"

What do extraterrestrials toast at bonfires?

Martian-mallows.

Police chief: "Your last two math teachers died from eating poisoned ham sandwiches, right?"

Suspect: "Well, yes..."

Police chief: "And your latest died from eating a poisoned peanut butter sandwich?"

Suspect: "Yes..."

Police chief: "Doesn't that seem *strange* to you?"

Suspect: "No. The last one was a vegetarian."

Crypt-Keeper: "I can't believe you told everybody I was stupid!"

Vault-Keeper: "I'm sorry! I didn't realize you were keeping it a secret."

Where do ghosts like to hang out?

On clotheslines.

Where does a vampire relax?

In a blood bath.

Why are girls who eat paste so obnoxious?

Because they are stuck-up.

Vault-Keeper: "What is worse than seeing a great white shark's fin in the water?"

Crypt-Keeper: "Seeing its tonsils."

HOW ABOUT NOT SEEING ITS FIN IN THE WATER?

What do you get when a truck runs over a hen?

Creamed chicken.

Vampire #1: "Why, oh *why*, does everyone hate me *so*?"

Vampire #2: "Because you're a pain in the neck!"

Why can't skeletons string tennis racquets?

Because it takes guts.

"Mommy, Mommy, I hate Timmy's guts!"
        "Be quiet and eat what's on your
        plate."

Why did the mortician leave a pail on the
sidewalk?
        So somebody would kick the
        bucket.

What has four legs and flies?
        A dead dog.

What goes ho-ho-ho-clonk?
        Santa Claus laughing his
        head off.

What is the most popular TV show
among ghouls?
        "Name That Tomb!"

What do murderers like best about driving?

Killing the engine.

What do you get if you cross the Atlantic on the Titanic?

Wet.

Crypt-Keeper: "So why are you wearing the neck brace?"

Vault-Keeper: "I got into an argument with this vampire, see, and he really chewed me out!"

What's red and mushy and found between a shark's teeth?

Slow swimmers.

Did you hear about the werewolf who went to the flea circus?

He stole the show.

Why did the mortician stay home from work?

Because she had a coffin fit.

What did the graverobber say to the beautiful corpse?

"I dig you."

"Mother...before I die...feed me...tuna casserole."

"Of course, son. I promise.
I...I never knew you *liked* my tuna casserole."

"I don't. It'll just...put me out...of my agony...sooner."

"Why were you sent home from school?"
"The girl next to me in class was smoking."
"But why were *you* sent home?"
"I set her on fire."

Witch: "I guess she was *really* coffin after that!"

Crypty: "No butts about it."

What do you call a fat vampire?
Draculard.

Vaulty: "Is it true that a vampire won't attack you if you carry a clove of garlic?"

Crypty: "It depends on how fast you can carry it!"

"Waiter! Waiter! Do you serve children?"

"Only when we're out of
everything else!"

When is it bad luck to be followed by a
black cat?

When you're a mouse.

"My mother has no nose."

"How does she smell?"

"Bad!"

Witch: "She's not the only one who smells bad."

Vaulty: "Crypty nose what you're talking about."

"Doctor, I've swallowed a lamb!"

"It should have no ill effect."

"But I feel so baaaad!"

Why do ghouls like to play cards in graveyards?

Because if someone doesn't show, they can always dig up another player.

What do calendars and prisoners on death row have in common?

Their days are numbered.

What do little ghosts drink in the summer?

Ghoul-ade.

Ogre #1: "I feel sick to my stomach."

Ogre #2: "It must be someone you ate."

How can you kill a killer bee?

With a BB gun.

What did the teacher say when her glass eye fell out?

"I've lost another pupil."

Why was the corpse absent from school?

Because he was feeling rotten.

A year after her waiter husband died, a woman attended a séance to contact his spirit. "George, come to me," cried his wife.

> And the image of George, in his waiter's uniform, appeared.

"Come to me, George!" she cried. "Please, come closer!"

> "I can't," wailed George. "That's not my table."

How can you stop a head cold from going to your chest?

> Tie a knot in your neck.

Why did the girl drink embalming fluid before going to the principal's office?

> So she'd keep a stiff upper lip.

Why was George Washington buried at Mount Vernon?

Because he was dead.

Why did the coroner dissect the nose?

To see what made it run.

What do you call a pile of dead ballerinas?

The *corpse de ballet*.

Witch: "Did you hear about the runner who wore white so that cars could see him at night?"

Vaulty: "No, what about him?"

Witch: "He was run over by a snowplow!"

Student: "Heavy-metal music *does* promote violence!"

Teacher: "Whatever makes you say that?"

Student: "Every time I play a Metallica album, my father hits me!"

How do you make a thin person fat?

> Push them off the roof of a building and they go *plump*.

Vault-Keeper: "Do you find Fran's face attractive?"

Crypt-Keeper: "I find it hard to read between the lines."

What do you get when you put a canary into a food processor?

> Shredded tweet.

"Mommy, Mommy! Daddy and I had so much fun at the beach! I buried Sally in the sand!"

"That's nice, Eddie. Next summer you can dig her up!"

What has two legs but cannot walk?

Half a dog.

"Teacher, I can't write on an empty stomach!"

"Then try a piece of paper, Ruth."

"Son, if you ever say that again, I'll give you a piece of my mind!"

"Sure, Dad. But can you spare it?"